FAMILY
COMMUNICATION

FAMILY COMMUNICATION

WILLIAM LEE CARTER, ED.D.

Rapha Publishing/Word, Inc.
Houston and Dallas, TX

Family Communication
by William Lee Carter, Ed.D. Copyright ©
Rapha Publishing/Word, Inc., 1991,
Houston and Dallas, TX.

Unless otherwise indicated, scripture
quotations are based on the NEW
AMERICAN STANDARD BIBLE,
copyright © The Lockman Foundation,
1960, 1962, 1963, 1968, 1971, 1972, 1973,
1975, 1977. Those indicated NIV are from
The New International Version, copyright ©
1983 by International Bible Society,
Zondervan Bible Publishers.

First Printing, 1991
ISBN: 0-945276-34-6
Printed in the United States of America

CONTENTS

TRYING TO COMMUNICATE

"Don't you know what I mean?" cried Melinda to her exasperated mother.

"No, I don't! You're not making any sense at all. I never understand what you say—and I don't think you understand yourself, either!"

Melinda refused to give in to her mother's lack of comprehension. She was determined to hammer away at her point. "Try to understand, Mom. When I said I was going to sneak out of the house this weekend and meet Trey and his friends, I was just kidding. I wouldn't do that and you know it!"

"That's the problem, Melinda. I *don't* know it! How do I know when you're kidding and when you're serious? What am I supposed to do, just stand back and let you do whatever you want with those no-good friends of yours? No way!"

"But Mom…"

"There's no use talking any further with me. You're grounded this weekend, and you can't talk your way out of it!"

Melinda stormed out of the room, screaming at her mother as she left. Alone in her bedroom, she cried at her failure to be understood by her mom. Simultaneously, her mother wept as she busied herself with household chores, wondering what she could do to more effectively get through to her daughter.

As I counsel children and their parents, I find myself repeatedly studying their communication patterns. I have become convinced that every emotion a child experiences is presented to his or her parents in some fashion. No feelings are withheld.

The parental role requires taking a leadership position in guiding family communication. Taking their cues from Mother and Dad, children express themselves through words, silence, action, rebellion, cooperation, physical illness, or other symbolic means. To effectively guide his or her child through the inevitable turbulence that accompanies childhood and adolescence, a parent must study the family's communication pattern so adjustments can be made to stimulate the emotional growth of the young person.

HOW CHILDREN COMMUNICATE

Meanings May Be Hidden

As I listen to children talk, I assume that beneath the apparent message they convey to me hides a greater wealth of valuable information. It will be of use to me, if only I will patiently wait for it to emerge.

I recall one of my daughters asking me one summer day, "Dad, will you be coming home for lunch today?" It was immediately apparent that she was not as interested in *my* schedule as she was in telling me *hers*.

"No, not today," I replied. I kept my gaze on her, nonverbally acknowledging the opportunity to reveal her secret to me.

"Well, that's OK. I'm going swimming with Kate today so I won't be here." Having made her announcement, she gave me a detailed description of the plans she and her friend had made.

When communicating with adults, children often show only the tip of the iceberg before revealing their full range of thoughts. As in my brief dialogue with my daughter, it is sometimes easy to recognize the child's need to talk further. At other times, children may more carefully mask their feelings with statements that are intended to test the adult's willingness to listen. Here are some examples of the way a child's words may hide a deeper meaning:

- "I hate school! All they do there is give you ridiculous work to do!" (*I'm feeling overwhelmed by the responsibilities I have.*)

- "They won't let me have a turn." (*I want to be treated as an equal to the older kids.*)

- "William is always in a bad mood. I never know what to expect from him." (*I worry that William's mood swings may be a sign that he doesn't like me.*)

- "I'm so depressed. I wish someone would tell me why." (*I think I know why I'm unhappy, but I'm afraid others won't understand me.*)

- "There's no use trying to please Dad. He's impossible!" (*I'd give anything if Dad and I had a better relationship.*)

Words mark only the beginning of what a child or teenager is attempting to convey. True communication requires looking beyond spoken words for additional information that reveals the full meaning of his or her statement.

Communication May Be Seen in Behavior

There is a purpose for everything we do. Behavior is not displayed simply at random. Often children feel one way, but act another way. By comparing the young person's words with his or her tone of voice, body movements, facial expressions, actions, or lifelessness, we frequently notice a discrepancy. For example, a boy may say he wants to be more cooperative with others, but his abrasive conduct betrays his stated intentions—or does it? I find that, in many instances, children who "talk" louder through behavior than through words are actually expressing a sense of fearfulness. Fear implies a feeling that pain or discomfort is right around the corner. As he demonstrates his emotions, a boy is often hoping that others will recognize his need for understanding. This scenario can happen with girls, too, of course. To appropriately communicate with children, we must peer at the world through their eyes so the response we offer will match their needs. Here are some examples of behavior patterns that carry hidden messages:

• Joel has just turned 16 and recently received his driver's license. When he enjoys a wild Friday night driving recklessly through town with his friends, his behavior communicates his need to be recognized by his peers as one who is entitled to freedom from the laws that govern others.

• Clinging to her mother as she entered school, 8-year-old Maria was expressing her uncertainty about her ability to live up to the expectations others had of her. Outwardly, she complained of feeling sick to her stomach.

• Although several of her close friends advised 15-year-old Sherry to abandon her empty relationship with her boyfriend, she stayed with him, even though she wanted other male friends. Her behavior was an expression of her dependance on a boyfriend to provide her a sense of worth.

• Rolling his eyes as his mother corrects him for the haphazard job he has done cleaning his room, Robert turns away from his mom and reluctantly continues to straighten his closet. As he works, he thinks of ways to subtly show his mother the contempt he has for her rules.

Communication breaks down when emphasis is placed on the behavior of the child with little emphasis on his or her unspoken needs. Many parents have told me, "I have punished my child every way I can think of to get her to quit acting as she does but nothing seems to get through to her." Conversely, children and teens have told me, "No matter how often I show my parents how I feel, they don't get the message. I'm ready to just give up."

A problem arises in our communication when we, as parents, attempt to provide information or direction to our children that fails to match their needs. The communique we send to them may be rich with wisdom, but if we are not accurately responding to their requirements, our helpful guidance will be interpreted by the children as evidence of another failed communication attempt.

Emotions May Be Used to Communicate

We are all emotional beings. Every emotion we experience is a God-given tool for fulfilling the personal, social, and spiritual needs in our lives. As we grow into adulthood, we learn to properly use our emotions to serve their intended purpose.

Due to their lack of experience, children have limited knowledge about the appropriate use of emotions. Through the guidance of their parents they can develop a greater understanding of their emotional makeup. Until they have been taught how to control

11

their emotions, they may use them predominantly as a way of communicating negative feelings. Examples of how children may communicate through emotional expressions are seen in the following illustrations:

• In everything he attempted to do, Billy somehow managed to make a mess of things. Although he was a bright boy, he struggled to maintain passing grades in school simply because he failed to complete many of his assignments. Even though he knew what his responsibilities were at home, he seldom completed his chores without prodding. When playing with his neighborhood friends, Billy frequently fought and argued. He seemed to do few things correctly. His behavior was an expression of the inadequacy he felt deep within himself.

• Immediately following the birth of his sister, 5-year-old Ricky was immensely proud of the new family member and constantly hovered over her in a protective fashion. As she grew older, however, Ricky began to feel left out. Jealousy prompted a change in Ricky's behavior. He became more aggressive toward others than he had ever been before. He whined and cried loudly when he did not get his way. He even began to wet his pants fairly often, despite several years of successful toilet training.

• Fourteen-year-old Angela constantly questioned the intelligence of all adults. Believing she had better judgment than most people, she disliked having to accept instructions from her superiors. She tended to be preoccupied with herself and ignored the needs of others. When she committed an error, she was quick to find an excuse for her mistake. Angela was consumed with the emotion of pride.

• Renee's family felt they had to "walk on eggshells" when she was present. An overly sensitive girl, Renee was quick to feel hurt by even the most harmless statements directed toward her. Her self-esteem was a wreck. She made frequent comments that devalued her worth as a person and when things went wrong, she was too willing to accept the blame. Guilt was the emotion that dominated Renee's behavior.

Children whose behavior is motivated by domineering emotions *want* to change. Without the judgment needed to make positive alterations, however, they may overstate their emotional needs, hoping that a more responsible adult will take charge. While there is no single way an emotion will manifest itself in childhood behavior, the parent can learn to recognize patterns of behavior that suggest a need for deeper communication.

ROADBLOCKS TO FAMILY COMMUNICATION

In a letter that contains wise guidance about our relationships with others, Paul tells his readers, "Let all bitterness and wrath and anger and clamor and slander be put away from you, along with all malice. And be kind to one another, tender-hearted, forgiving each other, just as God in Christ also has forgiven you" (Ephesians 4:31–32). These words can be fashioned into a framework for healthy family communication.

A primary responsibility of the parent is to develop an atmosphere in the home that encourages good communication. A healthy home environment should contain the elements Paul encourages: kindness, tenderheartedness (or sensitivity), and a forgiving spirit. Even when these elements are present, however, if harmful communication strategies are employed, the net result can be frustration for the entire family. Some of the more common, but preventable, causes of communication failure in a family are identified below:

• *Right words at the wrong time.* In communicating with others, timing is everything. Good communication not only involves an appropriate choice of words, but requires that those words be spoken at the appropriate time.

Once when my junior-high daughter asked me to allow her to join some friends at a social event, I told her no. She was upset with me and did not understand my reasoning. Later, when she heard that the party had gotten out of hand, she was able to hear the words I had to say: "Emily, when you asked me to go to that party I had an uneasy feeling because some of the other kids who were invited are not always well behaved. I didn't want you to be there if their behavior became too rowdy. I didn't think it would be in your best interest, even though I'm aware that you didn't trust my judgment at the time."

Convinced by a friend who attended the party that the behavior of several boys was crude, at best, Emily was willing to acknowledge the value of my parental decision. Had I gone into detail about my fears *before* the event, she would have labeled me as an overprotective dad and could have openly questioned my judgment. Good timing requires finding the appropriate opportunity to voice words the child needs to hear.

• *Overstatement of a valid point.* Shawn, a 13-year-old boy, showed me how repeated, though useful, information can result in blocked communication. The young man told me, "My mom is constantly telling me to keep up my grades in school. She says school means everything to my future. She's afraid I'll never make anything of myself so she keeps pushing me to do my best."

"I think you're convinced that your mother is right—you *do* need to do well in school," I responded, "but it must irritate you to hear the same thing repeatedly."

Shawn laughed. "It does, but I irritate my mom right back."

"How's that?" I asked.

"Simple. I do bad in school. It drives her up the wall!"

In this short conversation the boy provided several valuable insights that can teach us a lot about family communication. First, it is evident that he fully comprehended his mother's belief in the value of education. That point rang out loud and clear. Beyond that, however, Shawn suggested that he was able to look beyond his mother's verbal warning and sense her fear that he would not heed her good advice. Recognizing that Mom had taken his problem of poor school performance as her own, Shawn perceived his mother's overstatement of a valid point as an opportunity to become irresponsible.

In essence, Shawn believed his mother was communicating, *Shawn if you don't do well in your schoolwork, I'll have to bear responsibility for you*. Willing to wait until he was older to apply the wisdom of her warning, Shawn gave her ownership of a problem she did not want.

• *Lectures and sermons*. Like poor timing and overstatement, lectures and sermons can also strap a family's communication process. A mother told me that after giving her daughter a 15-minute lecture on why she was not allowed to go to an R–rated movie, the girl called her friend on the phone.

"She said 'no,'" the daughter told her friend.

"I said a whole lot more than 'no,'" explained the mother, "but all she heard was that one, two-letter word." What made Mom's

situation even more exasperating was the fact
that her daughter did not utter a single word
of response to the lecture.

Many children would identify parental
lectures as "clamor" as they examine the list
of relationship guidelines Paul gives in
Ephesians 4:31–32. James also warns against
the overuse of the tongue (James 3:1–4) and
suggests it is wise to bridle the tongue as a
way of teaching others. My general rule of
thumb when giving corrective instruction is
to complete the statement in the briefest time
possible.

Children have various ways of rejecting
the ideas we would teach them in our sermons.
Most often, they will "tune out" the adult and
possibly reject the opportunity for parental
guidance. By doing so, the child
communicates to the parent, *I do not want to
accept defeat, thus I refuse to acknowledge a
problem exists.*

A second, more blatant, form of rejecting
the parent's verbal counsel is to offer a

counter argument. One parent told me she realized her lectures to her son were fruitless when he responded with his own verbal tirade. "I didn't enjoy his verbal rambling at all. Then I realized he was only doing what he had seen me do. I learned a lot about the effect of my lectures on him through my own experience in listening."

• *Predicting the future.* A parent is the one person who can most accurately predict the likely behavior or emotion his or her child will display in a given situation. Because we live with our children and have the primary responsibility of teaching them social skills, we learn their strengths and weaknesses. A mother was heard to say, "I know my child so well that within a few minutes after she gets up in the morning, I can tell if it's going to be a good morning or a terrible morning. Nine times out of ten, I'm right."

But just try telling a child, "Dear, let's start out the day with a better attitude. I can tell you're in one of those moods when you get upset so easily." Then watch what happens. Your child may simply glare at you, virtually daring you to say one more word before he or she explodes. Or the child may prove you to be correct in your judgment of his or her mood and fulfill your prediction. Either way, it's a safe guess he or she will not receive your words as a valuable warning and then ask for further guidance.

Because children want to feel in control of their own behavior, parents' predictions are best left unstated. Recognizing their behavior as a cue to more closely monitor their actions, parents can avoid the struggle for control that can arise by predicting future behavior.

• *Accusations*. I have become increasingly convinced that children will tenaciously cling to their "right" to remain innocent until proven guilty. To test this hypothesis, a parent needs only to hurl an accusation toward a child and watch the reaction. As soon as the accused child feels personally threatened, he or she will quickly take a defensive posture to carefully guard against further harm from all aggressors. When this happens, all hope for meaningful dialogue ceases immediately.

Accusations usually begin with phrases such as, "I know...," "You always...," or "You never...." Accusations typically end in struggles for power with the child demonstrating his or her power over the authority figure by refusing to accept the allegations as valid. The child's unwillingness to confirm the adult's suspicion is a common power play.

In retaliation, the parent may feel the need to display parental power for fear of losing all influence over a potentially rebellious child. In general, dialogues containing accusatory remarks typically result in little positive change and a downward spiral of harmful emotions.

• ***Breaking confidence.*** Children will often say they don't share personal feelings and information because they're afraid others will learn of their imperfections. I know of no children, though, who do not want others to view their lives as they see them. It is natural to want to be known and understood fully. In the same way Christ encourages us to divulge our deepest thoughts in confidence to our heavenly Father (Matthew 6:6), we should assure our children that their private emotions are safe with us. Obviously, broadcasting a child's personal feelings and habits can damage communications, but so, too, can more subtle forms of disclosure, such as:

• Making well-intended, but unnecessary, jokes about personal information

• Basing disciplinary decisions on disclosed information

- Revealing information to others who have close family ties

- Using disclosed data as bargaining tools with the child

The dual role of confidant and authority figure often places the parent in an awkward position for making decisions in the child's best interest. A generalization about family relations states that children who can communicate with their parents with the security that information revealed will be dealt with in confidence are far more likely to develop a cooperative spirit. Young people who feel their trust in an adult has been violated will communicate through more subtle, often negative, behavioral patterns.

OUTCOMES OF FAILED COMMUNICATION

All family members are frustrated when communication efforts fail. Parents are at a loss to know how to give positive direction to a child who seems to be unappreciative. The child may refuse the leadership of his or her parents and make poor decisions due to youthful lack of judgment. The result may be misguided childhood behavior patterns that can ultimately harm the entire family. Several of the more common harmful behavior patterns are examined in the following pages.

Dishonesty in Relationships

Travis was a 12-year-old boy who freely admitted to me his tendency to lie to his parents. Quite candidly, he described how he kept his parents baffled by making up stories to suit his needs. For example, he would often deny knowledge of wrongdoing, even though it was obvious he was guilty. Even when he did tell the truth, he often failed to give a full account. When talking to me about his dishonest habits, Travis commented, "Why should I tell the truth? When I do, I always get into trouble."

I responded, "You mean as long as you keep getting into trouble, you're going to continue to hide the truth from your parents?"

"I sure am! Why would I want to tell them everything when I know I'm going to get busted?" he said.

Travis's manipulative way of communicating with his family members was a feeble attempt to express his deep insecurity about family relationships. He had learned that honesty in communication resulted in a negative payoff. By using deceit, he was actually sending his family a message. That message was one of fear.

I seldom see a dishonest child who feels comfortable about exhibiting a behavior pattern like Travis's. A certain degree of guilt accompanies the child's manipulative responses to his or her family members. In most cases, the child hopes the parents will recognize his or her emotional pain and adjust their communication style to make it easier to talk more openly.

Some of the more common ways a child may display dishonesty as a subtle form of communication include:

- Claiming ignorance of a situation that is potentially explosive
- Giving a half-hearted effort to assigned tasks
- Hiding the truth from parents rather than being helpful

- Claiming forgetfulness when asked to account for behavior
- Offering various accounts about an incident, each of which conflicts with the rest
- Diverting attention to others to avoid blame
- Turning the tables by claiming unfair treatment by the parent

In its most basic form, dishonesty is a communication ploy that is an attempt by the child to hide his or her true feelings. A deceitful pattern of behavior will continue if the child believes that honesty with others will be greeted with punishment or negative responses. If allowed to go unchecked, dishonesty may become a pervasive characteristic of the child that is hard to break. Prolonged, conflicted communication between child and parents can convince the young person that others cannot be trusted with his or her deepest thoughts.

Persistent Argumentative Stance

Argumentative children are hard to live with. They communicate the following message to their parents: *I know all there is to know. You can't teach me anything, so quit trying.*

It is common and normal for any child to be argumentative periodically. In fact, children need to know how to assert their independence. But continual arguments can break down communication, eventually causing family relationships to deteriorate.

Frequently, strained communication is one of the forces behind the argumentative child's behavior. By arguing with others, this child is trying vainly to bring some semblance of control to his or her world. Through conflict with the parents, the young person is overstating the belief that no one understands his or her feelings. The irony of the aggressive, argumentative behavior is that the use of force and overstatement make it difficult for parents to concentrate on the messages the child is trying to convey.

Note the following statements and behaviors and the implied messages that accompany them:

• Fifteen-year-old Corey stayed out until 1:00 A.M., even though his parents told him to be home by 11:00. When he was confronted with this rule violation, he retorted, "You're too strict anyway. None of my friends has to be in as early as I have to."

Implied message: *My relationship with you is so strained, I prefer to be with my friends as much as possible.*

• Eight-year-old Rebecca made yet another failing grade on a math test. Her mother, who knew she had the ability to be a strong student in math, scolded Rebecca for her poor performance. Storming out of the room, Rebecca shouted, "Everybody thinks

I'm a failure! I hate math. I'm going to keep on making Fs!"

Implied message: *I've lost faith in myself. I hope you haven't lost faith in me, too.*

• When asked to play the piano before a group of his mother's guests, Reggie began to cry and accused his mother of wanting to embarrass him. When his mother tried to talk him out of his feelings, Reggie pleaded, "Stop it, Mother! I don't want to play the piano for your friends!"

Implied message: *I lack confidence in myself. Please give me a reason to believe I am a capable person.*

Because of the vocal and often offensive way argumentative children express their emotions, they frequently feel lonely. Convinced that others are not able to see the world as they do, they overstate their emotional needs with the hope that their parents will read between the lines of their opposition. They want the understanding assurance from others that will give them personal confidence.

As communication improves between parent and child, the child invariably decreases his or her argumentative ways. Good communication teaches this child that force is no longer needed to be understood by others.

Self-Centeredness

Misunderstood children often become preoccupied with their own feelings. Believing that their parents are unable to view life from their vantage points, these children may retreat into their own private worlds of thought, refusing to accept the direction and guidance of more knowledgeable adults. They assume their own reasoning is better than that of the adults in their families who do not understand them. The result can be disastrous errors in judgment.

Leon: A Case Study. By the age of 10, Leon had become convinced that he was all alone with his thoughts. Feeling emotionally abandoned by his father, he disregarded everything the man told him. His father was a workaholic, seldom spending quality time at home with Leon. In Leon's thinking, his father could not possibly lead him in the right direction because he had not taken time to know the boy's internal thoughts.

In contrast, Leon saw his mother as an intrusive adult. He complained, "She's always on my case." Nothing he did seemed right to her. The lack of understanding he felt within his family encouraged him to make his own decisions about his needs, despite his youthful lack of wisdom.

Leon was forever procrastinating about his responsibilities. He convinced himself that it was not important to follow the rules others gave him. He simply wanted to glide effortlessly through life. He regarded school as a necessary evil and only did what was required of him to pass.

Leon dominated and even bullied his friends. He pushed his opinions on them and liked being in charge of whatever activity they were engaged in. Some of his friends began calling him "stuck up," but he ignored them. He thought he really was superior to most people. Leon was not a happy child, but he tried to convince himself that "the good life" was just around the corner.

At the root of Leon's dissatisfaction with himself was a lonely feeling of being misunderstood. Although he was only 10 years old, he lived in emotional isolation. His failed relationships at home had convinced him that other people could not be trusted. Although he attempted to take matters into his own hands and give direction to his young life, he was doomed to failure. Without the benefit of healthy communication in the home, he was without guidance.

Depression

Depression affects many people in our society. In fact, it is the most common form of emotional discomfort among all age groups. Depressed children typically feel alienated from others. In their isolation, they become convinced that their lives have little value. The failed communication of the depressed child's family reinforces his or her feelings of sadness and loneliness.

Through the communication children have with their parents, they come to interpret themselves in relation to others. Positive communication teaches children they are capable people who are able to make a contribution to their social world. Failed communication sends the message that something is lacking in their characters that makes them unable to find fulfillment.

Consider the following ways children may express their depressed feelings through words or behavior:

• Mark's mother was pleased when he decided to join the Cub Scouts. He had always been a reserved child who had refrained from joining social activities with other children. His mother hoped that in this organization he would meet other boys who would befriend him. To his mother's dismay, though, Mark quit after attending only three meetings. His explanation was, "No one even knew I was there."

• Lynn's teacher made an effort to be friendly to all her students and frequently gave them hugs and other tangible signs of positive regard. Lynn was one of the few students who failed to respond positively to the teacher's overtures. When asked to explain her reluctance to be befriended by her teacher, she quietly said, "I'm afraid to hug her. She might not really like me." Her chaotic family life had taught her to keep her distance from others.

• Randall's father happened to be outside when he saw the boy's playmate fall off his bicycle and hurt himself fairly badly. He was perplexed that Randall simply stood by without offering aid. When asked about his lack of concern, Randall stated, "I didn't think he wanted my help." The frequent criticism he had received throughout his childhood had convinced Randall he was not capable of rendering aid to others.

Communication among family members is a powerful force in shaping the behavioral qualities the child eventually displays. Healthy communication in a home convinces a child he or she has many positive capabilities. This belief can spur the child to relate to others through ways that are responsible and mature.

Misguided communication creates a feeling of doubt in a child. A doubtful child will take the inevitable negative circumstances of life and interpret them as evidence of his or her inability to make a difference in his social world. The result can be the development of behavior patterns that are both destructive to the child's self-concept and frustrating to his or her family.

PARENTAL GUIDELINES FOR FAMILY COMMUNICATION

Parents want to communicate openly and productively with their children. Many parents experience frustration and uncertainty about how and when to give children needed guidance. They become exasperated by offering wise counsel to a child who promptly rejects it and acts inappropriately.

Before discussing the specific communication needs of families, I would like to first emphasize that communication with a child can be effective only when that child clearly recognizes that the emotional environment of the family is safe. My own observations have

41

convinced me that, to a large degree, the behavior of the parents determines the quality of the atmosphere in the home. The relationship the parent cultivates with the child forms the basis for openness. The responses given to young people by their parents affects how they relate to others.

A prerequisite for family communication, then, is the development of parental behavior patterns that positively impact the home. A good communicator's most important qualities are:

- A sense of warmth and respect for the child

- A high degree of emotional security and stability

- An interest in others that allows alternative points of view

- A commitment to a democratic style of leadership

- The ability to separate emotions from behavior

- A healthy sense of humor

- A sensitivity to the needs and interests of the child

Parents who cultivate these characteristics are in an excellent position to groom a healthy communication pattern within the family. The communication techniques that follow help create a healthy home environment that promotes emotional growth and maturity.

Make Statements That Demonstrate Understanding

Proverbs 10:14 tells us, "Wise men store up knowledge, / But with the mouth of the foolish, ruin is at hand." I admire the wise counsel of Solomon, even though he is blunt in expressing his wisdom. The beauty of scriptural teaching is its wide application to a variety of individual and family needs. For example, this proverb can help parents remove one of the most difficult barriers to communication—the inappropriate timing of statements intended to provide guidance.

Earlier we identified poor timing as a hindrance to communication. We saw how poorly timed statements of guidance and explanation can be a turnoff to the child. But what *can* a parent say during a child's emotional display to keep the communication channels open? A brief conversation between a mother and her daughter demonstrates how a parent's understanding nature can positively impact such communication.

"I can't stand Mrs. Fleming!" complained Fran, speaking of her English teacher. "She gives us a test every single week, and they're hard!"

"Taking a hard test isn't your favorite thing to do, I'll bet," her mother responded, listening patiently.

"I'll say. The whole class is nervous on Thursdays because you never know what she'll put on the exam. Everybody really crams for her tests."

"I take it you're not the only one who dreads her tests. The whole class must worry about how they'll fare on her exams," the mother said.

"Yeah," continued Fran, "and when we get our test papers back, we all get nervous." There was a brief pause. "On today's test, I made a 76. That's the worst I've done all year."

Not wanting to impose additional guilt on her daughter, Mother responded, "That's disappointing. You were making an A in her class. A low grade will affect your average."

Unprepared to give up, Fran asserted, "Well, I may have lost my A average for now, but we still have several more tests before our report cards come out. There's still time to bring up my grade."

A wise mother had focused on her daughter's frustration. By demonstrating her understanding, the mother allowed Fran to come to an appropriate conclusion about how she would handle her school responsibilities in the near future. If Mother had immediately tried to pinpoint Fran's problem so she could offer her a solution or advice, she might have abruptly halted any meaningful dialogue. The conversation could have ended in a struggle for understanding by an exasperated child.

A related proverb teaches, "Wisdom rests in the heart of one who has understanding" (Proverbs 14:33). Adults, who have had greater opportunity than children to comprehend human traits, are expected to use their wisdom as a guide for family relationships. Applying this concept requires parents to display an understanding nature as an effective communication tool.

Make Effective Use of Confrontation

Certainly there are times in every family when a child must be squarely confronted with the consequences of his or her error or lack of judgment. But too often, the parent will employ confrontational communication in a negative way, such as pointing out discrepancies in the young person's behavior or way of thinking. Confrontation that is misused can cause a child to feel inadequate and can actually encourage further acts of irresponsibility. Then, in a twist of irony, the confrontation that was intended to push the child toward personal growth may result in either increased dependence on the parent or alienation that leads to hostility.

Confrontation may take two forms. Children can be confronted with discrepancies between their words and their behavior, or they may be confronted with information that provides an opportunity for further growth and understanding. Examples of situations in which confrontation might be needed include the following:

- Even though she had been told numerous times not to run in the house, 5-year-old

Tammy sprinted from her bedroom past her father into the living room.

- Concerned that her daughter did not recognize the arrogant tone of voice she was projecting, Mother felt a need to point out the effect of the girl's attitude on others.

- Jim's piano teacher gave him a break from piano lessons during the summer months, with the understanding that he would practice three times weekly during that time. Ignoring his teacher's admonition, Jim boasted, "I'll practice in August and she'll never know I took a vacation in June and July."

- Fifteen-year-old Ryan liked a girl named Michelle, but it was evident that she did not share the same affection for him. In his hope to win her over, Ryan made a nuisance of himself by frequently calling Michelle. His parents worried about the eventual harm that might strike their son as the result of his actions.

Discussing human relationships, Peter urges each of us to "show proper respect for everyone" (1 Peter 2:17, NIV). I believe parents have an obligation to their children to demonstrate respect for the young persons' emotions as the parents use confrontation as a communication tool. Respect for our children involves more than a recognition of their worth as persons. This concept includes the belief that even a child is capable of thinking competently and coming to appropriate conclusions about his or her needs in life. A parent shows respect for the child by refraining from judgmentalism, maintaining the child's sense of dignity, and appropriately assisting the child in growing toward maturity.

To build on the idea that effective communication involves parents using statements of understanding, we can say that confrontation is most constructive when it follows the demonstration of understanding. The relationship between parent and child positively impacts or, conversely, destroys the effect of a confrontive remark.

To successfully convince a struggling child, "You're only hurting yourself with your behavior. Nobody will take you seriously as long as you act like that," the parent must first be secure in his or her relationship with that child. We should recognize confrontive communication as a risk. For this risk to pay positive dividends, the parent must have first made his or her relationship with the child a priority.

A child who is confronted by an understanding parent is more likely to learn from the verbal reprimand, behavioral limitation, helpful criticism, or instructional guidance. Before deciding to confront the child, the adult must determine the child's ability to benefit from this form of communication, and then react accordingly.

Communicate through Your Actions

While parents are frequently cautioned that children observe their behavior as a guide for living, most of us find this truth to be difficult to remember. It is hard work to consistently present a positive example to the developing child. If most of us were truthful, we would have to admit it is easier to tell our children, "Do as I *say* and not as I *do*." I confess that I have seen the apostle Paul as somewhat arrogant as he tells his Corinthian followers, "I urge you to imitate me" (1 Corinthians 14:16, NIV). Yet, as we further study Paul's personality, we see that his statement was not a boast of arrogance, but a reflection of simple confidence. Recognizing that the understanding of the Corinthian people was infantile (1 Corinthians 3:1) in comparison to his own spiritual knowledge, he accepted the chore of nurturance and guidance as a part of his relationship to them. So, too, should we accept this role in our family position as parents.

It's true. The personal qualities of the parent communicate a strong message to the child. Examples of parents' positive characteristics and the nonverbal communication that can result include:

- Patience (*I trust you to learn from your mistakes.*)

- Emotional control (*Every emotion can be used productively if a healthy balance is achieved.*)

- Kindness (*You can trust me to keep your best interests in mind.*)

- Affection (*I will remind you of your worth as a person.*)

- Consistency (*The world you live in is predictable.*)

- Decisiveness (*Choose what is right and be properly assertive.*)

- Light-heartedness (*Enjoyment plays an important part of life.*)

- Democratic awareness (*Every person is capable of making a contribution.*)

- Respect (*Each of us has equal value.*)

Other, more harmful, characteristics can give a different set of messages. For example:

- Argumentativeness (*It is important to overpower others.*)

- Criticism (*You should always expect the worst to happen.*)

- Selfishness (*The needs of others can be ignored.*)

- Pride (*It is important to place yourself above others.*)

- Greed (*You can find true happiness in the accumulation of things.*)

- Immorality (*Gratify your own desires at the expense of others.*)

- Judgmentalism (*Nothing is ever good enough.*)

- Unreliability (*Others' needs are not important enough to be considered.*)

- Disinterest (*You are not important enough to recognize.*)

We would all like to send only positive messages through our actions. But being imperfect, we realize we err occasionally in the communication we convey through our behavior. When I counsel families, I often ask the children to offer their views on the positive and negative ways the parents communicate their views. Parents are surprised many times at the way their behavior is interpreted by their children.

I find it helpful for the parent to periodically solicit information of this sort from the child. We should recognize that the young person can offer insights on the effect our behavior has on family life. The child's perception of adult actions can benefit the parent in his or her role as family leader.

Use Communication As a Building Tool

One of the tasks of parenthood involves the building and shaping of the child's self-image. During the childhood and adolescent years the parent plays a central role in the way a young person learns to view himself or herself in the context of social surroundings. I believe communication is the most important tool the adult can use to assist the child in understanding himself or herself in a complete and positive sense.

An insightful, but chronically sad, 10-year-old boy named Gary once told me, "I know there are good and bad things about me. I want to be good most of time, but usually I'm not. Then I get mad at myself because I don't like being in trouble so much of the time. I guess I'm just bad."

As Gary and I talked, I encouraged him to tell me more about his opinion of himself and how he arrived at the conclusion that he was "bad." Although most children Gary's age have difficulty explaining a low sense of worth, this young fellow quickly told me, "Well, I get a lot more attention when I'm bad. When I'm good, my parents ignore me. But when I yell or do something wrong, my parents notice me. I guess I get punished so much that I think I'm bad, too."

From Gary's comments we can draw several conclusions about the way communication tools can be used to build a child's self-esteem. One of Gary's greatest needs was to feel understood by his parents. While he believed his parents fully recognized his faults, he was not convinced they had acknowledged his positive traits. Children equate listening with understanding. Often they will state that they feel good about themselves when they perceive that others have listened to them and have comprehended their emotional needs.

Related to the need to be understood is the child's need for regular affirmation of his goodness. Gary implied that when he behaved positively, he felt ignored. He surmised from the lack of attention he received that it is undesirable to be well behaved because good behavior receives no reward.

Gary's more subtle message was his feeling of helplessness about not knowing how to solicit positive comments from others. Through a lack of positive communication, he had not developed adequate social skills to equip him to get along successfully in his world.

The following guidelines may help you to successfully employ communication skills to build your child's sense of worth:

- Learn to "listen" to the hidden messages your child's behavior conveys.

- Actively identify the feelings and emotions you think your child experiences. Tell the child you are aware of these feelings and let him or her respond.

- Use statements that describe the desired behavior your child has displayed. "Gary, I like the way you got up quickly when I asked you to wash up for dinner" is more acceptable than a more general compliment such as, "Gary, you're such a good boy." He can more readily accept the first statement than the second comment.

- Use rewards such as prizes, extra privileges, or additional allowance. Couple these rewards with verbal praise, smiles, or physical affection. Gradually reduce the rewards so that social reinforcement is more commonly used.

- Look for an opportunity to provide a compliment or reward. As the child's behavior improves, increase your expectations of him or her.

- Communicate desired behaviors through your own actions. Remember, you're always on stage.

- Make a special commitment to spend 20 to 30 minutes of individual time with your child at least twice a week.

Paul advises us to "Let no unwholesome word proceed from your mouth, but only such a word as is good for edification according to the moment that it may give grace to those who hear" (Ephesians 4:29). Applying this communication guideline to the family, we can recognize the child's need to hear at least two times as many positive remarks from his parents on a daily basis than negative comments.

Application of healthy communication in the home can change the way children interpret themselves in relation to others. While inborn temperaments and personalities cannot be changed, they can be successfully shaped into a positive form. Children who feel deeply understood and are able to express themselves without fear of reprisal can develop stronger, healthier relationships with family members.

Editor's note

At Rapha, we believe that small groups can provide a nurturing and powerful environment to help people deal with real-life problems such as depression, grief, fear, eating disorders, chemical dependency, codependency, and all kinds of other relational and emotional difficulties. The warmth, honesty, and understanding in those groups helps us understand why we feel and act the way we do. And with the encouragement of others, we can take definitive steps toward healing and health for ourselves and our relationships.

Not all groups, however, provide this kind of "greenhouse" for growth. Some only perpetuate the guilt and loneliness by giving quick and superficial solutions to the deep and often complex problems in our lives.

We urge you to find a group of people in your church, or in a church near you, where the members provide acceptance, love, honesty, and encouragement. Rapha has many different books, workbooks, leader's guides, and types of training so that people in these groups can be nurtured in the love and grace of God and focused on sound biblical principles to help them experience healing and growth.

To obtain a free list of the materials we have available, please write to us at:

Rapha, Inc.
8876 Gulf Freeway, Suite 340
Houston, TX 77017

About the Author...

Dr. William Lee Carter is a licensed psychologist at Child Psychiatry Associates in Waco, Texas, a nationally certified school psychologist, and a consultant for Rapha, Inc., serving frequently as a speaker at Rapha conferences and seminars. He received his Doctor of Education degree from Baylor University in 1982. His practice involves consulting with school districts and counseling children, adolescents, and their families in both inpatient and outpatient settings. He and his wife, Julie, have three daughters, Emily,

Sarah, and Mary. He is the author of *The Parent–Child Connection, Teenage Rebellion*, and *Look Inside Your Child*.